Protect Us from All Anxiety
Meditations for the Depressed

William Burke

Drawings by
Mary Southard

ACTA
ASSISTING CHRISTIANS TO ACT
PUBLICATIONS

For Patricia, with love from her brother

My gratitude to Dr. Jonathan Kelly and Ms. Susanne Liles, R.N., of the Isaac Ray Center in Chicago, who reviewed these pages and offered helpful suggestions; to Dr. Joan Faloona of Christ Hospital, Oak Lawn, Illinois, who first read this book and gave me encouragement; to my loving sister, Mary Ellen, and to my family and friends, who had to learn as much about depression as I did; to my friend, Fr. Joseph Ruiz, who gave wisdom and strength when I badly needed both; to Colette McNicholas, who generously compensated for my computer ignorance; to the staffs and people of St. Cajetan Parish in Chicago and St. Ann Parish in Lansing, Illinois, for their sensitivity, their welcome humor, and their prayers; to the truly professional staff members of the Institute of Living, Hartford, Connecticut, who have led me and so many others back to mental health; and to Kevin, my roommate at the Institute, who amazed me by his courage.

Scripture quotations are the author's own free translation, based on years of pastoral usage and preaching.

Library of Congress Catalog Number: 98-73097
ISBN: 0-87946-184-5
Printed in the United States of America
02 01 00 99 98 5 4 3

Contents

Day

Epilogue

Introduction

Brothers and Sisters,

This is an unusual book, a fact I will be the first to admit. It is spiritual and personal, unlike many other worthwhile books about clinical depression. You may wonder why I wrote it this way, and I thought it best to explain.

Just a few years ago, I was—I thought—a happy and productive man. I was pastor of St. Cajetan Catholic Church in Chicago, a wonderful place with a feisty urban spirit and caring people. Halfway through my first six-year term as pastor, on a late August day, I was preparing for another busy year. My staff and I were about to hammer out our goals for the parish and for ourselves.

Then, seemingly without warning, I was blindsided by depression. My emotional life fell apart, and I entered a state of rage, humiliation, and despair. The pain was worse than I ever imagined it could be. Yet, bad as it was, my condition was eased by the immediate concern of my staff and family, by the understanding of a good friend, and by the professional and medical care I received. Within days, that love and attention prodded me to take the first steps on the road toward recovery.

Three months later, when I returned to my parish, I decided not to hide anything. In bulletin columns and homilies, I shared what had happened to me and urged those who felt depressed to seek counseling, which was available at our parish facilities. Within six months, before I left St. Cajetan's to take on the less stressful life of an associate pastor at another parish, *fifty* parishioners had shared their own stories of depression and recovery or had asked for help.

That is one reason I wrote this book—to try to help my fellow sufferers of depression. All fifty reflections are based on journal entries I made during my illness. It is my hope that the frankness I display in these meditations will act as an urgent plea to those who suffer with this illness: *Do not wait; seek immediate help!* Depression feeds on itself, and only honesty and soul-sharing, with the help of a counselor, can begin the healing—the return to light and joy.

I also wrote this book to praise God openly and in print. During all the hurt and the days of hopelessness, I discovered that God did not wait for me at the end of my illness; rather, God shared my grief with me all along the way, leading me to a new revelation of the divine reality and of myself. Those discoveries, I am convinced, could have been made in no other way. The psalmist was right: Even what seems to be darkness may be only "the shadow of his wings."

God bless you and heal you.

William Burke
Hometown, Illinois

Night

D-Day

*"Enough, then, of worrying about tomorrow.
Let tomorrow take care of itself. Today has
troubles enough of its own."*

Matthew 6:34

I look back now and much of it is still unclear to me:
why and how I became depressed. Was it mostly a
genetic thing? Do I blame my ineffectual thyroid? Was it
my perfectionistic behavior, trying to give 1000% to
everything all the time? Or was the cause as complex as
I am, as each human being is, with no two cases really
alike?

Unlike a lot of people who imperceptibly slide into
depression, I had an obvious D-Day: August 24, an awful
day that is branded in my memory. If there were any
bad omens in the preceding year, I didn't see them. It
was my third year as pastor, and the time seemed to be
flying by. I do remember worrying about not accomplish-
ing as much as I had hoped (and now I wonder what my
idea of "accomplish" was).

There was only one omen I could have read and
it happened the night before, August 23. I was on my

way home from a delightful day with friends at a Michigan lake, driving in the dark down Interstate 94. I suddenly began to feel clammy and light-headed, as if I were in a weird and frightening dream. The trucks roaring by took on the appearance of monsters crowding me off the road, as if there were no drivers at their wheels. I remember thinking, "What's happening to me?"

I slept fitfully that night, and as I said Mass the next morning I noticed that I felt *nothing* at all—no pleasure in the moment, no anticipation of the day, nothing. I began to panic. After Mass, when a staff member approached me, I nearly bit her head off. Then, five minutes later, during a routine phone conversation, I fell apart.

I was shocked, appalled, humiliated: This couldn't be happening! I learned later that no one who knew me well was really surprised, only deeply concerned. Had they been warning me, and I hadn't listened?

What did they see that I didn't?

Lord, how did I get so out of touch with myself? Don't let it happen to me again; help me heed the signs and people you send to warn me.

What Will I Say?

In God I take refuge; how can you say to me,
"Flee to the mountain like a bird"?

Psalm 11:1

What was I going to tell my parishioners?

My breakdown happened on a Friday, so that weekend there was scarcely time to put a statement together. From another parish where I was resting, I called in to report that I was "exhausted" and would return soon.

After my first day in therapy, however, it was obvious that I would not be back soon, for I was diagnosed as having "mild to moderate" depression. Though it further depressed me to think about it, I knew I would probably be going to a medical facility for extensive treatment. The parish would survive, of course; the staff was skilled, and my young associate was more mature than his years. But the question continued to plague me: What should I tell my parishioners?

I decided to tell them the truth. Why wouldn't I?

But counter advice flooded in: "There's a stigma

4

attached to depression; it can be dismissed as weakness. You don't want to go through that." "People don't have a right to know your private business. You're better off using exhaustion as your explanation." "If you admit to depression, people will be uncertain of you as a counselor or afraid to burden you with their own problems."

During this time, I read about the need for greater understanding of depression as an illness that affects millions of people of all ages. I read reports about wonderful new medications—Prozac, Paxil, Zoloft, and others—that help people get back on their feet and move beyond despair. I read about how those who suffer with depression need to be told the symptoms of the illness and urged to get the help they need. Were my parishioners—hard-working, urban, idealistic— any different from me in being vulnerable to this illness? How could I help them if I denied I was sick?

I sent out my announcement a week after I left the parish: "My dear people, I am suffering from depression. With God's help I will return as soon as I am healed. Please pray for me."

It was the right decision, Lord. Thank you.

The Basement

The older son said to his father, "For years now I have slaved for you. I never disobeyed one of your orders, yet you never gave me so much as a kid goat to celebrate with my friends."

Luke 15:29

My anger is a house. I'm on the first floor, with all the reasons for my anger catalogued, sorted, and filed, and there's even more room for storage on the second floor if I need it. I spend all day reviewing my files—justifying to myself again and again how right I am to be outraged, to seethe with resentment at the people in my life. Who could deny the truth of this overwhelming array of evidence?

But with counseling I begin to discover that the root of my rage is buried much deeper in me, way down below my consciousness, in terrible dark shadows I did not know existed and, therefore, could not acknowledge or confront: perceived humiliation as a child, emotional abandonment, serious betrayals of trust, the love I attempted that was spurned or ignored.

The source of my anger is in the basement of my house—and I'm afraid to go down there.

Lord, I don't have to go down there alone. My counselor, my dearest friends and family, and you *will turn on the light and go down with me.*

Loved Ones

"Martha, Martha, you are anxious and upset about many things. One thing only is necessary...."

Luke 10:41-42

On the darkest days of my depression, when the pain goes beyond pain into true agony, the thought of those I love makes things worse. The more intimate I am with people, the more I desperately worry for them.

I feel I am taking my loved ones down with me, drowning them in my own sorrows, wearing them out, using up all their powers of compassion, wearying them to death with my unending grief. It is one thing for them to see their children through the ups and downs of life, to help their friends through daily and ordinary crises, even to assist their aged parents with fevers and bedsores.

But to put up with my depression? It's like a bad movie with endless reels, an illness with no perceptible end in sight and progress so slow that at times it seems nonexistent. *I* know I will heal; *I* know this excruciating fog will lift. But do *they?* Will my family and friends still be there when I recover? Or will they have succumbed to the despair that even now tries to claim me?

I base my hope on—and cling to—these two truths:

* I cannot judge the strength of my loved ones. I have entered depression, where all fears are exaggerated.

* Those who love me are free human beings whom I cannot control. If I love them, I must let them be free to love me as they will. Even—especially— when I am sick.

Lord, if my loved ones don't deserve the consequences of my depression, neither do I. Help me truly love them by doing what I need to do to get well.

The Truth

Jesus took the blind man's hand and led him outside the village. Putting spittle on his eyes, he laid his hands on him and asked, "Can you see anything?"

Mark 8:23

If I do not attempt to control them and their care of me, and if I try not to underestimate their resiliency, is there anything more I can do for my loved ones, some way I can help them help me?

Yes. I can tell them the truth.

I may be tempted to lie, for example, regarding the amount and severity of my pain, for fear of depressing those I love. But if I attempt to tackle all this grief alone, I won't get well. I am a social animal; I need people; God heals me through them. They have to know how bad I feel if they are to understand my behavior, to know when I need more consideration or intimacy.

I may also be tempted—strangely enough—to hide the good days, to dismiss the bright spots as flukes instead of what they are: signs of hope. I can let my family and friends feel the sun when it shines in me. It will light their lives as well.

Besides sending the right signals to my friends and family, I gain another advantage in telling the truth. Looking reality straight in the eye has a healthy effect on my soul. It was by being unreal, by evading the truth, that I entered depression to begin with.

Lord, help me remember that the ancient enemy of humanity has not been called the "Father of Lies" for nothing! The truth may hurt, but over time it heals.

Tears

I am wearied with sighing;
Every night I flood my bed with weeping.
I drench my couch with my tears.

Psalm 6:7

D ear God, how many tears do I have?

There seems to be an internal sea behind my eyes. My fits of crying move me beyond embarrassment with my loved ones, beyond explaining and explaining—but how can I ever explain? This incessant grief is almost comic, but nothing comic has ever hurt so much. I'm afraid one day I may start crying and never be able to stop.

It is my illness that makes me think this way, as if I should apologize for my pain. My torment is real; I have a right to my tears. God gives them to me and to all sufferers to help us bear what feels unbearable.

I will not apologize for being human.

Tears heal, and I *want* to be well.

Man of Sorrows, take me with you beyond these
tears, beyond this cross, into new life.

Companion

When I wake up in the morning
(Especially in winter when it's dark
Outside and I can hear the wind complain)
I lie there dazed with sleep and wonder briefly
Where I am and what the date is, what I
Have to do—and then I suddenly
Remember. And I pray, "Oh God, I beg,
I plead with you; let this new day be different,
Let me feel better, please, only
A little better than before and then
I can have hope, I can hang on"—but even
As I pray, the old anxiety
Descends to stretch and claw my face, the dreaded
Sadness overwhelms my faint petition,
Bitterness brims over in my eyes.

With a soundless cry I look up at

The crucifix that watches over me,

The tender Christ from Mexico, with pinioned

Arms and painted wounds (yet which I know

Are real enough and deeper than my own)

Who has been up before me and embraced

My grief, my endless loss, my day.

Be my Light, Lord, when there is no light.

Denial

I am numbered with those who go down into
the Pit,
A person without strength.

C onversations with myself, over the course of my
life:

"Why is my leg throbbing?"

Because I leaned over too far on the ladder and fell.

I landed on my ankle.

"Oh."

"Why does my head feel like it's coming off?"

Because I ran down the stairs and tripped. I suffered a
concussion.

"Oh."

"Why do my emotions feel like they've been run
through with a knife?"

Because I worked and worried too much. I lost touch
with myself and entered depression.

But here there is no *"Oh"*—only a stunned, disbelieving silence.

Depression? *Me?*

Concussions and fractures I can understand, but depression is for those who can't cope with life, can't handle death, downsizing, or broken love affairs. "Depressed" is a label for weak people who can't "get a life" or "pull themselves together." I'm stronger than that, I know I am.

Aren't I?

No, I'm just a good and decent human being who must learn not to lean while on ladders, not to run down stairs, and not to ask of my mind and spirit more than God ever intended. Concussions, fractures, and depression are ways of getting my attention, perhaps even of saving my life.

Lord, the more I spend on denial the less time I'll spend on listening to you, to my counselor, and to loved ones...and getting well.

Lifesavers

*But a Samaritan who was journeying along
came on him and was moved to pity at the
sight. He approached him and dressed his
wounds, pouring in oil and wine.*

Luke 10:33-34

I have one of those plastic pill containers that is neatly
divided into seven small compartments—seven little
cubes, cheek to jowl, each holding a day's worth of
Zoloft and Desipramine. I feel chained to the things: the
oblong pill and the round pill—every day of the entire
year, every day a reminder that I am sick and need
help from pills to get out of bed, to eat, to want to do
anything at all.

One day, in a fury, I throw the container against
the wall and watch the pills scatter and bounce across
the bathroom floor.

I need to let out my anger, at least for one day.

But my resentment keeps me from seeing the
medications as friends, as lifesavers. They cannot cure
me, of course; a cure will come with time. Still, in the

flood-time of my illness, they hold me up so I can see the shore.

Master, scientists and medical specialists I do not even know are trying to help me. Do not let me refuse their help out of pride or self-pity. They, too, are part of your healing plan for me.

The "Damned Thing"

*There appeared in their synagogue a man with
an unclean spirit that shrieked, "What have
you to do with us, Jesus of Nazareth? Have you
come to destroy us? I know who you are—the
Holy One of God!" Jesus rebuked him sharply:
"Be quiet! Come out of the man!"*

Mark 1:23-25

Ambrose Bierce wrote a horror story about a fiendish animal that could not be seen. Bierce's hero kept a journal of his search for courage in facing this threat. The man's last journal entry was etched in sheer terror: "God help me! It's the 'Damned Thing!'"

I think about that as I stand in the safe haven of my bathroom and prepare to brush my teeth. I know I am growing slowly—so slowly—out of my depression. It takes longer now for the "Damned Thing" to lock in on me in the mornings. Today, though, it attacks again, viciously, as I put the toothpaste on the brush. I lay down the brush, lower my head. My eyes fill with tears. The dreaded litany sounds in my head: What's the use of getting up, of showering, of brushing my teeth? *For what?*

"God, help me," I pray—and God does. I say "No!" to the depression, out loud—and even louder—and I begin to brush my teeth again. The emotional pain is terrible, as always, but I have learned—I *know*—that to defeat depression I must keep on doing small everyday things—force myself to do them—in defiance of the "Damned Thing."

Until I win.

And I will.

God, when the enemy is full of strength, help me remember that you and I are stronger.

The Tree

Only in God be at rest, my soul, for from God
*   comes my hope.*
God only is my rock and my salvation, my
*   stronghold; I shall not be disturbed.*

                              Psalm 62:5-6

After lunch, I walk around the lovely tree-lined grounds of the Institute. Each tree bears a professionally made sign that gives the tree's name in both English and Latin. I have come to know each tree as a friend, someone I can count on to be there for me every day. I have learned all their names and salute them that way: "Hello, Tulip. Nice to see you, Sugar Gum."

Always, my walk ends at Bur Oak: a massively torsoed giant with stout limbs and slender branches that reach toward the heavens with open hands. I love this tree—his solidity, his permanence, his serene and majestic silence. He speaks quiet and peace to me, to one who has neither feeling within.

One day, when the pain within me is awful and I feel I am falling apart, I go up to Bur Oak and embrace him. I spread my arms around his trunk as far as they will go, and I hang on for dear life.

I don't care who sees.

O God, thank you for your strength. Help me hang on.

Toxic Shame

"Anyone who hears my words," Jesus said,
"and puts them into practice is like a wise man
who built his house on rock. When the rainy
season set in, the torrents came and the winds
blew and crashed against his house. It did not
collapse; it had been solidly built on rock."
Matthew 7:24-25

Toxic shame.

The phrase sounds awful, and the reality is worse.
It is a condition of self-loathing, of primal emptiness
where my healthy pride should be. In toxic shame, my
whole sense of self is a mansion built on a raft, a house
of cards, a curtain hiding the Wizard of Oz. Remove the
fancy shell over which I have frantically labored—and I
feel naked and worthless.

And terrified.

How is this shame born? Perhaps somewhere in
my family history someone begins using children to
meet his or her needs...and so the children's own needs
for dignity, value, and a sense of self go unmet. When
these children grow up and become parents, the gro-

tesque pattern is repeated. The shame of having no inherent worth becomes internalized, unspoken, unacknowledged: the basis of a horribly backward world. And so, I, offspring of this unhealthiness, feel forced to *earn* my worth: to seek applause and praise abroad, instead of hugs and kisses at home.

But then one day the raft tips over, the cards collapse, the Wizard's curtain flies open. I have no more energy or will to maintain the charade, and I am revealed within its ruins—naked, worthless, terrified.

And depressed.

Lord, I have been busy my whole life meeting expectations that you never set.

Perfectionist

Two men went up to the temple to pray; one was a Pharisee, the other a tax collector. The Pharisee, with head unbowed, prayed in this fashion: "I give you thanks, O God, that I am not like the rest of men."

Luke 18:10-11

I am a perfectionist, which I should declare as honestly as a member of AA announces "I am an alcoholic." A perfectionist is ill, trying desperately to live an impossible life. And if you want to torment a perfectionist, ask him or her to do what my spiritual director asked me to do: keep a journal.

Agony, pure and stark—unmitigated horror! For there in my own (imperfect) handwriting is a daily record of incompetence: stupid ideas, half-baked resolutions, pathetic attempts at insight, even a log of my mostly pedestrian dreams. No sooner do I finish an entry than I read it over with disgust. My anger at this ridiculous exercise grows by the day.

"I'm a lousy journal keeper—or whatever you call it," I tell my spiritual director with some heat. "I can't seem to get the hang of it—whatever the hell you're supposed to do."

"Supposed to do?" he asks, expressionless.

"Come on," I tell him. "You wouldn't ask me to do this goofy thing if you didn't have a reason. What am I *supposed* to be learning?"

"Why do you think you're so bad at it?" he asks.

"Look at it," I say. "Look at this page, for instance, from last week. I honestly can't believe I wrote that. It's like it was written by somebody else."

"Maybe it was," he replies.

There is a long silence in the room.

Lord, I hate the imperfect in me. I despise it. I want to hide it. Which means I hate, despise, and want to hide me. Yet you love me. Something's got to give.

See Spot Run

"Can any of you by worrying add a moment to your life span?"

Luke 12:25

See the priest work hard all week for the honor and glory of God.

See the priest run here and there, wield a phone, and write letters—*all at the same time*—and finish twelve other things before lunch.

See the priest fume and fret on Friday because during the week he forgot to do three REALLY IMPORTANT things, or ran out of time. Maybe he should have skipped his day off to get the stupid things done somehow.

See the priest on Sunday speak from the heart—and his seventeenth draft—about St. John's wonderful words (are you listening out there?): "Love then consists in this, not that we have loved God, but that God has loved us" (1 John 4:10).

See the priest the following Wednesday leave piles of work on his desk and run downtown for a long meeting because the archdiocese has a priest shortage ...and he wants to help.

Lord, see the priest pray, "Protect us, Lord, from all anxiety," and then not let you protect him.

The Leper

"All the Father gives me shall come to me; no one who comes will I ever reject."

John 6:37

During this time, the gospels take on greater meaning for me. I find myself identifying with those who come to Jesus to be healed—especially with the leper. He is afraid of imposing on Jesus, as if he feels he is not really worthy of Jesus' attention.

"If you *want* to," the leper says, "you can cure me" (Mark 1:40).

Jesus is stunned by the pathetic condition of the man and by the forlorn tone of his request. All of the villagers, at the sight of the diseased man, have run away; the leper kneels alone in his humiliation. Jesus' reply to the man is from the heart: "Of course I want to!" (Mark 1:41). He stretches out his hand to touch the disfigured skin, the troubled soul—and he heals the man.

I don't know why, but my illness makes me feel as if God isn't interested in me. I know better—in my brain, in my memory of God's past mercy to me. But my emotions sabotage me. In my prayer I swing from feeling nothing at all to wanting to hide from God, as if my depression is deserved—some deep uncleanness in me risen to the surface of my life—and repulsive.

Like the leper I plead with Jesus: "If you want to, you can cure me." But in my nightmare world he turns away from me.

For now, I must rely on what I know, not what I feel. I will say it out loud, I will write it down: "Jesus never turns anyone away, never. When I am well I will feel what I already know, that all through my illness his love embraced my uncleanness, my self-loathing, to make me whole."

Perhaps, Lord, you will wish to touch me through someone close to me. Help me to recognize you.

Face in the Crowd

His disciples said to him, "You can see how
this crowd hems you in, yet you ask, 'Who
touched me?'"

Mark 5:31

Another gospel story I have come to love is usually
referred to as the "Woman with the Blood Flow"
(Mark 5:24-34). Mark doesn't tell us what causes the
woman's bleeding—perhaps it is cancer of the uterus—
but she is desperate to touch Jesus' clothing and so be
healed. She wants no more than that: a touch of the
hem of his cloak, for she is a woman in a man's world
and thinks herself unworthy of Jesus' notice.

I see her in my mind, and I feel for her. The bleeding makes her ritually unclean, and for that reason she
doesn't want Jesus to touch her and become unclean
himself. Perhaps she thinks all her grief is "God's will" for
her and punishment for her sins. If so, she seeks to re-
main faceless before the Holy.

I am like her, as I am like the leper. I don't want to
bother God; I don't want God to look at me right now.
My depression isolates me, drives me into a shell,

screens me from God and from anyone else I fear might confirm the little I think of myself.

And yet I will never be cured unless I leave the shell, unless I reach out to the one who can heal me. I need courage, and Mark tells me to find it with *people*: family, friends, counselors, and the everyday people of my life and career. With "the crowd" pressing toward Jesus, I can approach him unafraid. They—healthier than I—can bear me with them toward the Lord.

Lord, I see you wheeling about in the crowd, asking for me. I can't believe (I can't feel) that you love me that much. But you sent Mark—and all the people in my life—to tell me so.

The Sheep Pool

Have pity on me, O God, for I am languishing;
Heal me, O God, for my body is in terror;
My soul, too, is utterly terrified;
But you, O God...how long?

Psalm 6:2-3

How long?

Maybe the worst part of my depression is the feeling that it will never end, that I will always be this wretched, soul-dry nomad adrift in dead space. The terror that comes from thinking that! I have gagged on that fear, sat with my head in my hands, my whole body shaking.

For the first time, ever, I understand why a person would *want* to die.

But I *don't* want to die! I want to *be well!* Dear God, do you hear me?

I open the gospels, read John 5:2-5, and I am there:

*Now in Jerusalem by the Sheep Pool there is
a place with the Hebrew name Bethesda. Its
five porticoes were crowded with sick
people lying there blind, lame, or disabled,
waiting for the movement of the water.
There was one man who had been sick for
thirty-eight years.*

Thirty-eight years! How did he ever bear it?

Perhaps John—as he so often does—is writing
figuratively here. Perhaps the man's thirty-eight years of
suffering are the length and breadth of all our illnesses.
For when we are in agony, a day becomes a year, a
night an eternity.

I lie on my mat at the Sheep Pool.

I wait. I pray.

Time drags on.

---

*Oh Master, when will you come by? Do you know
where I am?*

The Sick Man

God has heard the sound of my weeping;
God has accepted my prayer.
                                    Psalm 6:9-10

There was one man who had been sick for thirty-eight years. Jesus, who knew he had been sick a long time, said when he saw him lying there, "Do you want to be healed?" "Sir," the sick man answered, "I do not have anyone to plunge me into the pool once the water has been stirred up. By the time I get there, someone else has gone in ahead of me." Jesus said to him, "Stand up! Pick up your mat and walk!" The man was immediately cured; he picked up his mat and began to walk (John 5:5-9).

I enter this reading as John invites me to, and I find great consolation here.

Jesus knows I am sick, has known since my nightmare began. I am not alone, abandoned, cut off from his love. I cannot feel his presence but he is at my side, and my fears begin to ease.

"Do you want to be healed?"

I know what Jesus means when he asks me that: he refers to the work I must do with him to escape depression. This illness has strong, deep roots, stretching all the way down into my childhood. If I want to be healed I must be honest and open about my pain, hiding nothing—not from him, not from my counselors.

"I do not have anyone," says the sick man. But *I* do! I have my family, my friends, my parishioners—all showering me with affection and support. They are the arms of Christ embracing me; they are his voice calming my spirit. They do not understand my illness, but they will bear with me for as long as it takes—until I am whole.

Jesus says to the sick man, "Stand up! Pick up your mat and walk!"

I wait for that day, and it will come.

I am physically able, Lord, to pick up my mat and walk. But I see no reason to. It is my will that is crippled and needs your touch.

Holiday Spirit

The Christmas holidays are tough. All around me I see and hear people having a great time: laughing, sharing stories, seemingly at ease with themselves and with others. Why don't I feel that way? It's as if I'm spoiling everyone's fun, dampening the atmosphere for those around me because I cannot feel joy. I feel only fear at this new year's coming, fear that it will bring more of the agony I have known for so long.

That fear is my illness speaking, cherishing defeatist words such as "same" and "more" and "agony." One step I can take now—this holiday season—is to think and speak positive words such as "hope," "growth," and "healing." These are wonderful words and they speak the truth: This will be a new year for me, too. I *am* growing and I *am* moving toward health, because God has not abandoned me. This coming year God will help me climb out of the darkness, step by step (even as I am careful not to take too many steps at one time). The One who has always loved me will support me when I falter.

We will get there, together.

Father, when I cannot feel your love, reach me through hope. This year, as never before, I will depend on you.

The Thorn

Truly you have formed my inmost being;
You knit me in my mother's womb.
I give you thanks that I am fearfully,
*   wonderfully made.*

Psalm 139:13-14

Screened from the main walk, he sits behind a bush on the grounds of the Institute and is the center-piece of a little fountain. It took me a while to discover him—there is such shadow over his small world. He is a Greek boy, about eight years old, cast in stone and verdigris. He wears only a headband and is breathtakingly beautiful. His fountain appears neglected, but that does not seem to bother him.

What does bother him, though, is a thorn in the sole of his right foot, no doubt picked up in a race. His right ankle resting on his left knee, he bends over the thorn in furious concentration. He will endure in this contest, too, I feel, and remove both thorn and pain.

As I pass by each day, he sits preoccupied, lost in the business of extraction. The boy is a lesson for me, for all who suffer with depression. He is not the thorn; he is not his pain. The accident was not his fault but is merely a fact to be dealt with. His wound in no way affects his worth, his identity, his goodness before God and the world.

Depression tells me the opposite, that I am always at fault, the wound *is* me, the awful feelings I experience are an accurate summary of my value. Worse: Depression makes me think the pain will never end, the wound will never heal.

But that is a lie, the dark brooding of my illness. I will not listen to the lie. The wound *will* heal, my depression *will* lift. Prayer and counseling, time and love, and God's power *will* win the day.

The thorn will come out.

Divine Sculptor, you look at all the works of your hands, and they are beautiful—as I am.

The Cistern

God reached out from on high and grasped me;
God drew me out of the deep waters.

Psalm 18:16

It must be true of any illness: the difficulty of talking about it. Where does honesty leave off and self-pity begin? When does candor become false humility? Someone once said: "A bore is someone who, when you ask how he is, tells you."

I'm afraid of coming across as someone looking for sympathy, when all I really want is a fellow traveler— someone who will understand, even if he or she has no advice to offer.

Recently, a friend cut me off at the knees with his comment: "Depression, huh? Well, enjoy the rest. I'm too busy to be depressed"—as if I were copping out or deliberately neglecting myself and my job!

Perhaps I might have told him and others about the cistern into which depression flings you. You stand groggily at the bottom, up to your ankles in muck. You look up, and the opening of the cistern seems to be miles and miles above you. There are no ropes, no rungs, and the walls are slimy with moisture. There are no handholds at all. The walls seem to be slowly closing in on you, the feeble daylight fading.

But worse—much worse—you see heads appear above, peering down at you. They are people you know and love, and they say, "What are you doing down there? Come on up." But they lower no rope, they offer no solution. They speak again, this time with faintly disguised irritation: "You've got to help yourself, you know. Snap out of it. We can't wait forever."

You shout in rage, "I can't get out," but they seem not to hear. The loneliness, the terrible isolation—the terror closes in.

By why speak about the cistern? How could anyone understand?

My suffering is not precious, Lord, it is not special. Help me share it. There is someone you will send to listen.

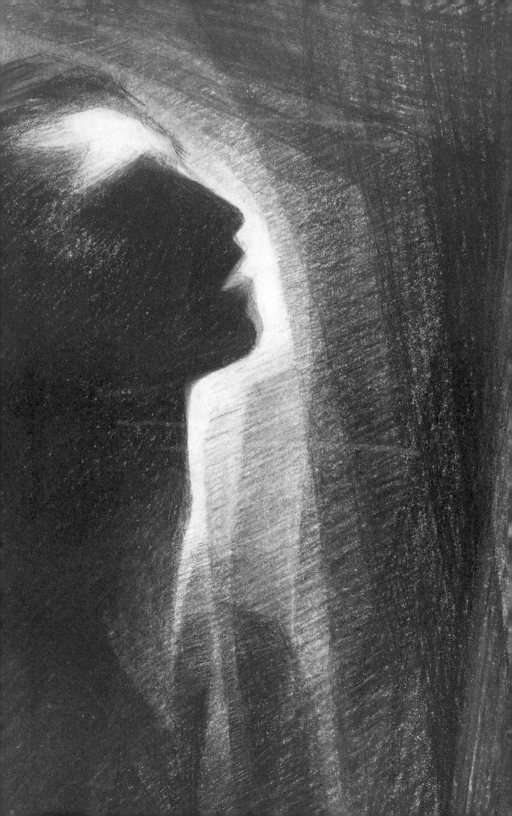

"Eloi, Eloi"

"My God, my God, why have you abandoned me?"

Mark 15:34

I have heard Jesus' mournful, shattering cry from the cross explained away so many times by preachers, homilists, Scripture scholars, and people hastening to reassure me that the Son of God could never be depressed.

Why don't they stop? Why don't they go away and let him cry, for himself and for me?

My God, I will cling to trust in you as Jesus did, even if by my fingertips.

Dawn

Counseling

"It's like a man," Jesus said, "who sets out on a long journey."

Mark 13:34

I seldom use the word "journey." I talk about taking "trips" or having an "experience" or being part of a "process." The word "journey" sounds faintly epic to me, a trek someone such as Odysseus would undertake.

But when I enter the counseling center for the first time, I know I am on a journey, and the thought scares me. Where will the journey end, and how far will I have to go to be healed? I have already been diagnosed with "mild to moderate" depression, and those words are unwelcome enough. What if this coming self-revelation leads me into quicksand, into an emotional hell I can't escape?

A friend who suffers depression told me my illness might get worse before it gets better, and I didn't understand. I resented the statement, and I resented him for making it. Why should my illness get worse when I am so desperate to be healed and get back to my life?

The center's hallways are gray, as I guessed they

would be. My counselor's office is spartan, as if he had moved in a mere five minutes before I arrived. My resentment grows. I don't want to be in counseling; I feel humiliated both as a man and as a professional.

If a journey begins with a single step, the first step is one I expected: a questionnaire. The counselor smooths out his standard form and begins to ask me biographical data. I fidget with restlessness and anxiety. Can't we skip all this and go immediately to some sage advice, some concrete remedies?

"Parents alive?" he asks.

No, both dead, cancer and heart disease.

"Brothers and sisters?"

Yes, one brother, one sister, both doing well. And...uh...my younger sister is dead.

"Cause of death?"

I pause.

Suicide.

"Why did you pause?" the counselor asks.

Stay with me, Lord. I don't know where this road is taking me.

The Cistern Revisited

God set me free in the open, and rescued me.
Psalm 18:19

How do I escape the cistern?

To escape depression I first have to talk about it, and that goes much against my male grain. I can open up with close friends, but admitting a need for professional counseling means I am clinically ill—and I hate to confront that fact. It makes me feel childish and stupid.

But when I do confront it, the cistern seems shallower, the opening closer.

As my counselor and I explore possible reasons for my illness, I feel the great fear of the unknown that many people with depression have written about. The last frontier is not space or the ocean floor, but the self. It is territory we can enter *not* wanting to know. But I do want to know myself! I want to be well.

And suddenly I see rungs, where I had seen none before, leading up from the bottom of the cistern.

After initial failures with medication, I grow increasingly angry and desperate. Why won't the "wonder drugs" work for me? For a while I refuse them altogether. Then the wisdom of my friends and my doctors prevails, and I try again. We finally discover the right medications, the proper dosage.

Strong arms reach over the wall of the cistern and pull me out.

I am still shaky from the experience, but I am back among the living. I panic easily, but I do not fall apart. I still need courage to socialize, to speak in public, to believe in the future that God has created for me—but the kindness of others has rekindled my hope.

When I go back, the cistern isn't there. I find only a shallow indentation in the ground.

I will come to other wells, Lord, prisons for other people. Help me know what to say then, how to extend a strong right arm.

First Step

Jesus asked him, "What do you want me to do for you?" "Rabboni," the blind man said, "I want to see."

Mark 10:51

She came into the room quietly, as if afraid of intruding. It was her first day, you could tell. Our support group had already begun its session, but we stopped to welcome her.

She sat down and looked around at us. In the silence, she smoothed her skirt, adjusted her purse. We were used to silences; she was not.

"I don't know why I'm here," she said suddenly. "I'm not depressed."

Most of us just smiled and nodded, but one man laughed out loud.

"I'm *not*," she said, glaring at him.

"Of course you're depressed," he said gently. "It's in your face, your walk, the way you sat down."

"But I don't want to be depressed!" she cried.

"Ah," he said, "good. That's the first step."

Oh God, sometimes I've lost ground, and lost hope. If I need to take the "first step" again, help me do it. It's the only way to the final step: freedom.

Demon

"A kingdom torn by strife," Jesus said, "is headed for its downfall."

Matthew 12:25

In Jesus' time, people thought in terms of tribe and nation, and particularly in terms of family. In a sense, you were who your kinsfolk were. Their opinion was essential in determining your worth, your pride, your shame. It was a time long before Freud and Jung, the ego and the id, and the idolization of the individual.

Which makes one of Jesus' parables all the more startling:

"When an unclean spirit departs from a man, it roams through arid wastes, searching for a place of rest and finding none. Then it says, 'I will go back where I came from,' and returns to find the dwelling unoccupied, though swept and tidied now. Off it goes again to bring back with it this time seven spirits more evil than itself. They move in and settle there. Thus the last state of that man becomes worse than the first" (Matthew 12:43-45).

One of the most fearful yet indispensable moments in my therapy as a person suffering depression is when I realize that I hold the keys to my own healing. I can choose to settle for an inadequate "cure," relying on my medication to get me to a level of relief, never probing into my anger or fear to find what has really brought on my illness. It would be so easy to make this lesser choice because I yearn so much for surcease from my pain.

But then my unnamed "demon" may come back in a ferocious mood, untamed, more devastating than ever ("seven spirits more evil than itself"). I must face the pain it takes to expose my demon now, to give him a name, and to root out his cause.

So I begin to fight the real fight for my mental health.

Jesus, you said the truth about myself would set me free. Strengthen me to believe you, to trust you, friend at my side.

Beautiful Morning

My soul waits for God,
More than sentinels wait for the dawn.
Psalm 130:6

I look out at the snow, newly fallen, five or six inches. It's dawn, a Saturday. No traffic and no footprints mar the beauty of the perfect white landscape. The dark undersides of the evergreen branches add character and dimension to the flawless scene. Only the dimpled tracks of a raccoon or cat show me that life has been up and about before me.

I see all this, and I feel nothing. My mind tells me this is a winter Eden, and my logic runs like a child from one window to the next, telling of the glazed perfection of a downspout, the dazzle of an icicle. But my emotions refuse to respond, to feel anything at all. They are momentarily numb. Perversely, I am grateful, because when my emotions do awaken they will return to their obsession with my pain.

But I have learned—my counselors helped me see—that my healing takes place slowly, step by step, moment by moment. Until my emotions are whole and I can feel again the thrill of beauty, I will be content with what my eyes and my mind tell me. I *know* that what I behold is wonderful. That will have to do for now.

Soon, when I am healed, I will go back in my memory to this moment and be able to say with joy, "It *was* a beautiful day, wasn't it!"

Master, you have made me so complex—like yourself. When one part of me won't respond, teach me to make do with another.

The Question

I've been in counseling for several weeks, and I am well into the love-hate phase of being a client. Talking about real issues in my life, looking closely at real behavior: It's exhilarating. I am not evading anything—so far as I know. I am trying to get at the causes underlying my illness. Why have I entered depression? The answer will suggest a way out.

But exhilaration or not, I am also experiencing real terror. In my profession I am usually the counselor, not the client. It is always somebody else's life we explore. I am safe in the confessional or behind my desk. Here, I am not; it's *my* life we're discussing. And I have the free and fearsome choice to pursue matters as far as I want, to know the truth, whatever it costs. I am deeply afraid.

But I must continue, I tell myself. I don't want to be sick.

The counselor sits in his chair, slightly tipped toward the wall. I wonder if his body language indicates professional distance or just plain boredom. But again and again he startles me by recalling what I said—sometimes hours or weeks ago—and probing it. He confronts me with matters I have skimmed past, making me go back and see and understand.

Patterns emerge in my life, sometimes healthy, sometimes neurotic: all clues. Gradually my fear gives way to humility. I am a human being; it is all right to go on searching. I am ill, but I can build my healing on my strengths.

I feel I am getting better, but we are at a cross-roads, and the counselor knows it. Sitting directly opposite me, he says, "You're a complex person, and we've made some good progress. But you've given me only a nice thick frame for your problem...very interesting, but only the frame." He leans toward me. "Are you hiding anything? Right now? Something you're very much afraid of?"

Oh God, how little faith I have in you! Do I really think I'll lose you within myself—where you already wait for me?

"This Above All"

"You shall love your neighbor, as you love yourself."

Mark 12:31

It was a dream, and as always with my dreams
I have forgotten most details.
But not the ending.
I remember how it ends.
I play a role upon a stage—I think it's Hamlet—
And the audience is screened from me by spotlights.
I see only darkness where "reality" has come
To favor fantasy, quite willing to trade places.
But no matter what I do, the part goes badly.
Those who sit in darkness damn my efforts,
Cry out rude remarks,
Find laughter in my grief, and groan
At my carefully polished wordplay.
Panic builds in me, bursts into rage at them
Who boo now, catcall.
I have never been so shamed.

Mercifully, the play is done, the lights go up;
The audience is discovered: one man only,
And I recognize the jeering mouth,
The cold and mocking eyes I find
Within my mirror every morning.

---

*Divine Lover, let me look into your eyes instead,
and learn the truth of my worth.*

R-E-S-P-E-C-T

Jesus looked at him with love.
Mark 10:21

At least twice a year I get requests from teachers in
our school to "speak to the children about respect." The requests are born of those interminable days
in November or March when the weather is wretched,
the teachers feel like wardens, and the kids are sure
they're in Sing Sing for life. As a result, the students begin
to take out their frustrations on their fellow students.

Respect, I tell the kids, is hard, because we'd
rather *get* respect than *give* it. Respecting another does
not mean merely "letting somebody else alone" or
admitting that "someone is different from me and that's
O.K." Respect means to "look again" at a person without the blinders of prejudice or the perverse desire to
control.

I write on the blackboard, "Respecting you
means I approve of you as a human being, I allow you
your space, I permit you your unique role in this world."
Then I ask the kids, "What's wrong with this statement?"

Seeing only furrowed brows, I explain. "Respect has nothing to do with my approval of you as a person or my allowance of your existence or my permission for you to have value. That language stinks! Your worth does not depend on my judgment; God has already given you beauty and dignity. When I respect you, I *acknowledge* the worth that is already there, even if I dislike you or disapprove of your conduct."

This is deep stuff for young people, but after I give them some examples and we discuss what's been happening in school, they seem to get the idea. The question is: Do I?

"Physician, heal yourself." When I reflect on my own words, I wonder: Do I respect *myself*? Have I learned to distinguish between the harmful conduct I sometimes engage in, the mistakes I make, and *me*?

If I am so slow in recovering from depression, could it be because I don't approve of myself, won't allow myself to breathe, won't permit myself to be the human being God loves...and respects?

Teacher, I still try to earn your love—and my own—and that's such a disaster for my mental health. Please be patient with me. I'm a slow learner.

Prodigal Son

By means of many such parables he taught them the message in a way they could understand.

Mark 4:33

A s I grow older, I love the parables of Jesus more and more. I think that's because most of the problems in my life are not completely resolvable; they're messy, complex, mysterious. I pursue one lead— and find even more of the puzzle. And the main puzzle is myself.

Parables usually begin with "a certain man" or "a certain woman" on an undetermined day, and end nowhere in particular. That's because I, the reader or listener, must continue the story for myself. Parables are like paintings whose weary artist hands me the brush to finish. They share that blunt but subtle style that Mark uses when, at the end of his gospel, he runs out of words and tells me tacitly: "You take it from here."

I think of all that when I read the parable about the two sons in Luke's beautiful fifteenth chapter. Luke begins the chapter with lost sheep and lost coins, and then proceeds to lost sons—*two* of them. For both children are "lost": the younger, "prodigal" son to folly and greed, the older, "good" boy to resentment.

The older son is my mirror image. He would never think of insulting his father as viciously and stupidly as his brother does, nor would he publicly disgrace his family that way. No, he is seemingly content with being the firstborn, the good example, the George Bailey who sacrifices his own dreams for twice the work and little praise. In the process, however, he stuffs down so much anger and bitterness that he finally explodes in rage at his father and brother, thereby isolating himself. "Come and get me if you want to love me," he cries.

Which is what I cry to God and to my family in my worst moments, while I yearn—ache!—to be my prodigal brother and get a hug, a kiss, a party.

But you do embrace me, Lord. I just don't feel it. Your music does play for me. I just don't hear it.

Magnificent Mile

A time to weep, and a time to laugh,
A time to mourn, and a time to dance.

Ecclesiastes 3:4

One spring morning I was walking down Chicago's North Michigan Avenue—the "Magnificent Mile"—and all of a sudden it *did* look magnificent. The boisterous architecture towered up into the warm, welcome sun; flags rippled in the clear, rain-washed light; the newly planted tulips in their storefront beds tossed heads of tangerine, lambent yellow, and lipstick red—riotous on their straw-green poles. On the facades of buildings, brass and copper fixtures mirrored my face—and I saw that I was grinning!

For a person with depression, a moment such as that is a taste of heaven, an ecstatic reprieve from the leaden anxiety, the unending sadness. I danced around like a man set loose on parole. Did they understand— my fellow sufferers from depression who happened to see me that day? Did they envy me my good fortune?

That fortune ran out at 1:30 that afternoon. The brass and copper dulled, the colors faded, the dance ground to a halt. As suddenly as it had come, the feeling of health and joy vanished. I plunged back into the gray of sidewalks and clouds and concrete, my face set in its usual tight, fraudulent smile. And when I could pray, I forced out the words in grief:

"Dear God, where did that joy come from?

"Dear God, where did it go?"

It was a glimpse of my future, Lord, a sign of hope from you. Healing is coming, my medication is helping me—as you are helping me, always.

Upper Hand

"You will suffer in the world," Jesus said. "But have confidence! I have overcome the world."
                                                                    John 16:33

M y counselor is being transferred to another city, and I dread losing him. He has helped me immeasurably. Our relationship is in no way parent to child; rather, it's more like learned brother to needy brother, wise friend to one temporarily misguided.

During our last session, he says, "I believe depression will be a chronic problem for you. Can you be at peace with that?"

No, I can't! Chronic? You mean, never going away?

"Not quite," he says. "But I believe it will always be a battle for you because of your personality and your family history. And when I say 'battle,' I mean a battle you can win."

But what about medication and what I've learned in cognitive therapy? I thought I had an illness that could be healed!

"Healing doesn't necessarily mean it will disappear altogether," he says. "It can mean that you know how to deal with it, how to control it, how to keep it in perspective." He smiles. "I believe if you lost your depression entirely, you would also lose your creativity and possibly your compassion. I'd say that's too great a loss. Depression is the dark side of your gifts. Don't be afraid of it. You can keep the upper hand."

Since then, I have come to know that he was right. I can keep the upper hand if I accept my humanity as God accepts it, and if I work within it, not against it. Counselors can help me see where a balanced life lies, and God and I can take it from there.

Be my champion, Lord.

The Debate

"Fear is useless. What is needed is trust."

Mark 5:36

I have received an invitation to a graduation party. I know the kid; high school wasn't easy for him. But he has his own genius at art, at music, at just being himself—a funky sweetness that will bring joy to those he meets.

I want to go to the party. But the interior debate that is now so much a part of me begins again: Fear versus Risk.

FEAR: There's no disgrace in staying home. You're ill. Socializing is extremely hard for you right now. Take one step at a time.

RISK: I know all your excuses, Fear, and they won't help me be healed. I've got to keep communicating, learning how to hold my own. Yes, one step at a time, but hiding out is not a step at all.

FEAR: Shall I remind you of the last party, your pathetic attempts to smile, to pretend you were having a good time?

RISK: I was trying! I'm not saying it wasn't hard.

FEAR: Hard? Your smile was practically painted on; everything irritated you. Admit it, you were sorry you went. You felt stared at. Every bit of conversation was an effort.

RISK: What are you telling me, to give up completely? Depression delights in isolation, in self-pity, in anger nurtured and brooded over. Difficult as it is, mingling with people helps me stay real.

FEAR: Does staying "real" mean drinking half a bottle of wine just to keep from shaking?

RISK: That was a mistake, another form of hiding out. And you know that!

FEAR: You're pushing yourself, just as you always do. That's how you got sick.

RISK: Nice try, but this pushing is different; it's making myself do what I must do to get well. I need people, I need them right now. Just being with them will help me.

Lord, the invitation reads, "Regrets only." I don't want those words to describe my life.

Angel

The afternoon group sessions at the Institute have ended. The lounge area is empty except for myself and the woman who is crying. I feel sorry for her so I stay, sitting next to her on the couch.

In front of us on a low table are a box of candy and a bouquet of flowers. They are gifts for her from all of us in her group because this is her last day in therapy with us.

The woman says she is ready, but I wonder. She seems so sad and irresolute. She takes a tissue from a small packet and wipes her eyes.

"I know I've got to do it," she says suddenly. "I just can't go on talking about it. I've got to face my life— but oh God, it's so hard." She bends over and her crying deepens. I place my arm across her shoulders and just wait with her.

I don't know what to say that hasn't already

been suggested to her by her group and by her therapist. The divorce has been ugly, with her husband claiming that her chronic depression leaves her an unfit mother for their child. She faces a court battle she isn't sure she can win.

The woman fumbles with her purse, withdraws something, and hands it to me.

"Here," she says, "before I forget again. You weren't here the other day when I gave these out to our group. This one is yours." It's a papier-mache angel, exquisitely clad in lace and bright cloth. "I make them as a kind of hobby," she says as she gives a small laugh. "Crazy, huh? But they keep me from going completely nuts."

She takes the flowers and candy, gets up, and turns toward me. "Thank you, Bill," she says. "You were kind." And she walks off down the hall.

When she is gone, I look again at the angel. It is a miniature work of art, the angel's mouth a delicate round "O" of surprise or joy.

Or is it pain?

Lord, may we both feel the strength of your "angels" in our lives.

Dry Bones

*O my people, I will open your graves, and have
you rise from them.*

Ezekiel 37:12

I am rereading one of my favorite stories from the
prophets, Ezekiel: The Valley of the Dry Bones (chapter
37). Suddenly, I discover that the story is my own.

Somewhere in the past, Israel fights a great battle
in this valley, a fierce encounter with many casualties—
and Israel loses. Because of the need for a hasty retreat
and because of the cruelty of the enemy, the Israelites
cannot decently bury their dead. Shallowly dug holes
and a thin covering of dirt must suffice to inter the
bodies. Their sad chore done, the Israelites desert the
battlefield in despair.

Years later, the prophet Ezekiel—an eccentric
genius of a seer—walks through the valley and sees
everywhere the bones of the dead warriors bleaching in
the sun. "And they were very dry," he notes. The soldiers
are dead beyond dead: no muscle or sinew, no flesh or
skin. Bone is separated from its neighbor bone. The
scene is one of overwhelming loneliness and despon-
dency.

For Ezekiel, the battlefield and the bones speak eloquently about the state of his exiled people. They foresee no future for themselves, there is no parole from God's punishment and their own shame. "Our bones are dried up, our hope is lost, we are clean cut off."

And yet it is the supposed Punisher who thunders to Ezekiel: "Son of man, can these bones live?"

I, too, have known an exile: an isolation from myself, from my bleached-bone emotions, from intimacy with those I love. In my illness, I have shied away from a God I perceived to be wrathful and remote, a God who had turned away from me. The pain of this exile has been unbearable at times, for it is of the nature of depression to seem endless.

And yet I believe that my Creator lives. I believe that my Creator wills to breathe new life into me, to have me stand on my feet, a proud and loving man once again.

God's new creation has already begun in the care I am receiving. I must have faith until I feel that new life stir.

Son of God, can my bones live? Let it be soon.

Loving

"You are worth more than many sparrows."
Matthew 10:31

When I was in high school I had a pet parakeet. The little creature became a fantastic friend. I was big and surly and full of self-loathing and knew I was completely unlovable, but the little bird loved me anyway.

When I came home from school each day, sour and complaining after the endless bus ride, the bird would fly to meet me—he never stayed in his cage. He was full of news and gossip and questions—all in "bird-speak," of course—and he would run back and forth on my shoulder, ecstatic to see me.

When I would put a beer pretzel in my mouth, the parakeet would sit on the other end of the pretzel, and we'd both chew away until I'd start laughing and he'd drop off with a squawk. When I would sit at my desk and try to study, he'd sit on my book and look up at me as if to say, "Why study when we can play?" He would then proceed to take my homework page in his beak, run to the edge of the desk, and drop it. "Hey!" I'd say, but he'd bide his time and then do it again. When I would play the piano, he'd hang off the top of the sheet music until he and the music tumbled.

More than anything else, my pet wanted to share affection. Landing on my shoulder, he'd run up to my mouth and lisp, "Gimme a kiss," and wait for me to make a suitable smacking sound for him.

Shortly after I became a high school senior, my parakeet died of pneumonia, and I raged over his death for days. Being an "adult" male, I couldn't cry in public, so I wept when I was alone. The loss was devastating. Sitting at the kitchen table one day while my mother made dinner, I said suddenly and savagely, "I wish I had never loved him at all."

My mother replied, not turning from the stove, "Loving is always better than not loving."

Father, love me strongly now so that I can love again. Do not let me discount the good I have already done.

The Lord's Table

*"Take the fatted calf and kill it. Let us eat and
celebrate because this child of mine was dead
and has come back to life."*

Luke 15:23-24

Depression has foods it loves to feast on: self-pity,
shame, despair, isolationism, the stubborn refusal
to be helped or even to acknowledge the illness. When
so fed, depression intensifies all these feelings. But there
is another delicacy it craves and finds in some way in all
of its victims: perfectionism.

What a poisonous attitude toward life I choose
when I try to be "perfect," when I cannot live with my
mistakes or even admit them! It is impossible to live
"perfectly," and the very attempt makes me ill or builds
on my already existing illness. Actually, perfectionism is
my very human but pathetic attempt to *create* my
worth, since I believe I cannot possibly have any worth
apart from my own efforts. From this misperception I
spiral downwards. My shame feeds into denial and
pretense, and I take my place at the banquet of misery.

This is a toxic way to live, certain death to my

spirit. There is another table I am invited to, however, with healthier food—and I can come as I am. The Lord is host, and the main course is unconditional love.

How hungry am I?

My Gracious Host, sit me down, please, and feed me with your wisdom. Some day I will understand and dine nowhere else.

The List

While he was still a long way off, his father caught sight of him and was deeply moved. He ran out to meet him, threw his arms around his neck, and kissed him.

Luke 15:20

list here all the things I have to do today to earn God's love:

———————————————————

That white space is so consoling, Lord! I can dry my tears with it if I want.

Day

Not a Clue

But some seed fell on good ground, grew up,
and yielded grain a hundredfold.

Luke 8:8

A fter three months away, I return to my parish:
better, but not "cured."

Before I entered the frightening world of depression, I did not have a clue about how serious the illness was or what it could possibly feel like. In my earlier years I had done my "homework" as a minister by reading books and articles about depression; I attended seminars on mental illness; I even attempted to counsel persons suffering with depression until they could obtain medical help. But through all my exposure to the theory and pain of depression, I supposed the illness to be something like "the blues" or a bad, rainy Monday—only somewhat worse.

A rainy Monday, indeed! I find my ignorance incredible now, especially since my own beloved younger sister committed suicide. I realize how hard she must have labored not to lose the tenacious, inbred love of life we all have. She must have been in such agony, but I—her older brother—didn't understand.

Recently, a prominent man declared, "I would rather have every bone in my body broken than suffer depression again, because I know which would hurt worse." I take it he gained his awareness as I did.

I try to remember all this when my family, friends, and colleagues ask me how I'm doing. I feel the awkwardness of explaining because I know they can't understand—not really—any more than I can understand the pain of leukemia or the dark of blindness. We stand outside one another's sorrows, and wonder.

But I accept people's inquiries as signs of love, which they are, for I badly need the comfort they give.

Through their faces, Lord, their words, their hugs, and touches, I feel your own embrace. I praise you for your love and theirs.

Limits

"Where your treasure is, there your heart is also."

Matthew 6:21

It's called "hypothyroidism," and it's an illness that can create intense fatigue and lead people into depression, as it led me. In my case, however, it wasn't the illness itself that did the greater harm to me, but my reaction to being ill.

Hypothyroidism is caused by an underactive thyroid. Severe forms of the malady condemn the sufferer to be among the walking dead. Being a stubborn male and loath to visit doctors, I was practically comatose by the time I asked for medical help. I was put on a supplement, Synthroid, which brings most people back to normal.

Most, but not me. My finicky body returned to about 80% full power—then it stalled. As a result, I tried to resume my life, with all its demands and stresses, missing 20% of my energy. I hated that feeling of weakness, so I pushed ahead—using adrenaline and anger to fuel me. I went on doing all the work I used to do—and more—to express my resentment.

I did that for almost twenty years, until depression stopped me cold.

A wiser man now, I look back and understand. My sense of worth was so bound up in my work that to sacrifice any part of it would have meant diminishing my value in my own eyes and, I thought, in the eyes of people whose opinion mattered to me. I must have sensed I was taking a risk, but I judged that my "self-esteem" was worth it.

It wasn't. I chose not to accept my limits, and I paid dearly for that decision. Now I look with alarm at friends and acquaintances who are choosing to live the frantic lifestyle I once lived, and I wonder how to warn them—and whether they would listen.

Master, draw us all—the ones who labor and are overburdened—to yourself, and teach us to let go.

Dear Friend

She is a dear friend—and she happens to be very beautiful. So when we go out to a restaurant for dinner, I sense people wondering about us. "What's that old guy doing with *her*?"

Phooey, let them wonder!

After we talk about parish life, family life, her job, her new "romantic interest," movies, and books, we're content to ponder the dessert menu together. Suddenly she asks, "What's it like?"

"What?"

"You know. Your...illness."

"Depression?"

We've managed to avoid this topic, so I don't know if I want to talk about it now. I've been feeling good just being with her.

"Why?"

"I just want to know. I guess I want to understand better."

I debate with myself for a moment, then I tell her: incidents, feelings, the horrible days, the tolerable days. I use whatever images I can think of. I stop when I sense my anxiety building, like a dragon disturbed in its cave.

"Do you understand?" I ask her.

She says nothing at first, looking pained. She puts her hand over mine.

"No," she says. "I'm sorry. I've...just never felt that way."

For a moment I feel the perfect fool. But the shame passes, the acute ache of loneliness.

For I am glad she doesn't understand.

May she never understand.

Master, I have your understanding. Let it be meat and drink for me, as is the love of my friends.

Michael

They that hope in God will renew their
strength,
They will soar as with eagles' wings.
Isaiah 40:31

In June of 1976, I baptized the seventh child of dear friends of mine. The child was named Michael, and because the family had previously "adopted" me as "Uncle Bill," I was chosen to be Michael's godfather. The boy grew up fussed over, maybe spoiled, and much loved, as "babies" of the family often are.

Three years ago, in January, Michael was walking home from Sunday Mass with his girl friend. He was a graceful athlete and enjoyed "kidding around."

"Watch," he told his friend. "I'm Superman," and he dove into a snowbank. Underneath the snow was a core of solid ice that did not yield. Michael broke his neck at vertebra C4.

For a frightening few days we feared that Michael might not live, and then that he would be completely paralyzed. But by God's mercy—along with Michael's steely grit and the genius of his physicians and therapists—my godson graduated from beds and braces to wheelchairs and walkers in five months' time. Finally, he was able to stand upright and shuffle forward with a cane. He was cheered on by his friends and by the indefatigable love and support of his parents, brothers, and sisters.

In August, I encountered my own paralysis, but my illness was in my mind, not my body. As I struggled with depression, Michael continued to overcome his physical injury. He grew in strength and confidence, beating all odds, amazing his caregivers.

In December, as he and I continued to recover from our afflictions, we celebrated Michael's victory with a Mass at his parish church. Michael walked in—and walked out afterwards—on his own.

Neither Michael nor I will ever forget the last three years, and yet I know which of us has faced the greater challenge, scaled the higher mountain. I am Michael's godfather, his "uncle," and his elder; yet he has reversed all this and has become my mentor.

Let young and old praise you, Lord, for your goodness in our time of trial.

Anger

The heart knows its own bitterness,
And its joy no one else shares.
Proverbs 14:10

I have just finished hearing confessions in anticipation of Easter. The parish liturgy staff crafted a thoughtful prayer service: the Scriptures were illuminative, and the examination of conscience rang true. Both the divine word and the human word suggested many ways for wounded people to approach our merciful God.

But now I sit in the sacristy, still in my alb, thinking about the individual confessions I just heard. For people have just deluged me with multiple variations of my own problem: *anger.* Anger is confessed more than theft, pride, profane use of God's name, or sexual sins. On and on it goes: impatience, bitterness, feelings of betrayal and revenge, resentment, rage. The scarlet letter "A" is not for adultery; it's for anger.

Where does this sea of disquiet come from? Why are so many people so angry? When I pursue this topic with people, young and old alike, they get hostile: "Well, if you lived my life, Father...," "If you had to put up with what I do...," "If you had to live or work with...," "If you had a spouse/child, Father, you'd understand." Anger is always *somebody else's fault* or it's due to some *unexpected event*—as if we human beings are not free to choose our response but must always opt for outrage.

In such cases, of course, the "sin" of anger becomes nominal, since the penitent pleads "just cause."

When I become skilled at excusing my anger, I can expect no healing, no exit from my covert and overt depression. For I do not really want a cure. I embrace my anger, even enjoy it.

God is left holding the gift of peace, unopened.

"Bless me Father, for I have sinned." That's what I say, Lord: I have sinned.

Blame

"Peace I leave with you," Jesus said, "my peace I give to you. Not as the world gives peace, do I give it to you."

John 14:27

The residue of all the anger I hear in the confessional remains with me, like a stench in my clothing.

God gave us anger as a natural emotion to be used honestly, directly, forthrightly—while we search for understanding and resolution. But unhealthy anger is exactly that: noxious, a response that feeds on itself, avoiding resolution in favor of perverse delight in someone else's (perceived) wrong. Blame is "fun" and excuses us from action.

Sometimes, thank God, a penitent's voice becomes softer and humbler as the person owns up to unhealthy anger. But just as often, the voice becomes a hiss, an oral knife slicing away at the accused. When I suggest seeking counseling to control the anger, or at least pursuing in prayer the more basic reasons for such rage, there is silence or a quick request for a penance. The person wants only to be heard, not healed.

I, too, have luxuriated in blame, directing my anger at everyone and everything because I was afraid to go inside myself and find out what was wrong.

With God's help, I have found—am still finding, still discovering, still uncovering—the more remote areas of my pain and resentment. Perhaps that is why I now grow so sad in the confessional when I listen to angry people. I'm listening to myself.

How easy it is, Lord, to pray for peace—and yet be reluctant to accept it, because your peace would change my life.

Letting Go

*"Do not let your hearts be troubled," Jesus
said. "Have faith in God, and faith in me."*
John 14:1

I preach on the weekend following confessions—
following the epidemic of confessed anger—and I
wonder what I can say that will help. What I want to say
is simple: "Let go! Let God have all your anger, your
bitterness, your blaming. Let it all go, a flood tide of toxin
from your hearts. Let it all go to God, who can easily
absorb it. Give it to the Creator, the Transformer, the
Alchemist. And once you do that, think of the love you
can bring to the world, the peace you can authenti-
cally share! For anger imprisons, and now you'll be free.
Your beauty and energy for life will find new expres-
sion!"

Let go, let God!—a creed which is true on many
levels.

Those of us who suffer depression find it especially
hard—and especially urgent—to let go of anger. Depression wounds our very selves, and anger feeds depression. Many times, through the confessional grill or

face to face, I encounter a person who is in the grip of depression and doesn't know it. But I recognize the posturing, the denial, the fantasy life. And I grieve as for a fellow traveler in grief.

It is so easy to hang on to our fierceness, to lash out at others because we can't find our way inside ourselves (and if we did, we would pale at what we find there). That's why "letting go" is basically a matter of trust in God, who never abandons us. It may hurt like hell before we're done, but this hell is not a place of eternal loss. It is the place Jesus once visited to let us know we are not alone.

As so many have done before me, Lord, help me follow you and not look back.

"The One Whom You Love"

Jesus called loudly, "Lazarus, come out!"
John 11:43

I hear him, but I don't come out,
Preferring dark and peacefulness,
 where I belong.
Outside, where he and all who love me
 go on beating on my tomb,
Anemones are blooming, and red poppies grow
 in lush and shimmering grass.
I do not grow or feel or care, I am
 much more than four days dead.
There is no hope for me,
 why don't they go away,
 I try to tell them with my tears:
"Why must you make such noise?"

They grunt and sweat and push aside the rock
And he unwinds my linen strips
And stills my protest with his kiss.

103

So toddler-wise, to cautious cheering,

Lazarus comes out, but I delay my party

As I turn and stare into my tomb,

And wonder why I went in there.

Batter my heart, Three-Personed God, and come in to seize me when I don't respond. I give you leave.

The Key

And he told them another parable.
Matthew 13:24

It was late spring as a certain man set out on his first
hiking expedition into the Rocky Mountains. As he and
his three friends made their way up a steep trail, they
drank in the intoxicating beauty of the wildflowers, the
mad roar of the frigid stream that darted under and
over their path, the color and song of birds they had
never seen before. They passed through forests heavy
with the scent of pine, and became dizzy with pleasure.

When the man stopped to tighten the laces of his
boots, his friends moved on ahead into more rugged
territory. They made their way through a narrow part of
the trail that was hedged in by massive boulders, part of
a low-lying range of rock. As the man ran to catch up
with his friends, he found a massive wall, with a single
door in it, stretched between the boulders. He gaped at
the wall and tried the door. It was locked.

The man looked about, but there seemed no
way around the boulders except through the door.
What was it doing here? He called out to his friends,

whose voices were muffled and faint. He put his ear to the door and heard one of them say, "What are you waiting for? Let's go!"

"There's no key!" the man shouted back, "and the door's locked!" He wrestled with the door, pounded on the door—but it didn't budge. "They're going to leave me," he thought, "and I'll be alone up here." He panicked and beat his fists on the door even harder. Still there was no movement—and he could no longer hear his friends. The man looked back down the trail but couldn't remember how he had come up. The paths went in all directions.

As darkness gradually fell, the man sank to the base of the door and wept, the night sounds terrifying him. He prayed desperately, deeply, more honestly than he had ever prayed in his life. But the door would not move; the knob would not turn.

Dawn came, and the man woke—cold, stiff, and drugged with despair. With a frantic plea to God, he looked up at the door—and there was a key in the doorknob!

Unbelieving, he rose, preparing himself for failure. He turned the key, the doorknob revolved, the door swung open.

There, a few yards ahead, his friends sat talking. They turned and looked at him.

"Where have you been?" one asked, laughing.

"Lost in the bushes?"

"The door," the man said weakly, wiping the tear stains from his face. "I couldn't get through the door."

The others glanced at one another, then stared at him curiously. "What door?"

The man glared at his friends, turned to point out the door, and froze in disbelief.

There was no door, only the wide open passage, the pine needles beneath undisturbed.

Master, you are the Way, the Truth about me, my very Life.

Sick Call

"The gift you have received, give as a gift."
Matthew 10:8

When I was in the hospital fifteen years ago for thyroid tests, I sat in my room bored and restless. When my secretary called and told me that eight of our parishioners were also patients in that hospital, I got their names and room numbers and, for the first time in my life, I visited the sick in my bathrobe.

The people were at first astonished, and then seemed delighted to see me. I couldn't help but notice that our conversation levels were far more at ease and personal than they usually were when I made my visits in clerical clothing. The patients and I were now co-sufferers, and that shared state seemed to create a new world of openness between us.

I am no more eager than the next person to experience pain or illness, but I must admit that the few times I have known physical or mental suffering I have gained an insight into myself and others that I would not have gained otherwise. Perhaps after I have failed to acquire wisdom in any other way, God sends me a cross to make sure I learn what I need to know.

This cross of depression has been no different. In fact, it has been enormously instructive. I have learned the hard way how misguided some of my past conduct has been. I have also learned how painful—ungodly awful—depression can be. I want to remember that when I meet people who suffer from the illness, and suffer worse than I did. I pray that God will help me to be more understanding and compassionate with those who experience it.

As it is now, my fellow sufferers of depression and I can reach out to one another in any elevator, church, or restaurant by passionately discussing Zoloft, cognitive therapy, vitamin supplements, and group sessions—sometimes with pure sympathy, often with rueful laughter.

If this is how I gain understanding, Lord, so be it. (But strengthen me when I change my mind!)

"Into Your Hands"

Jesus uttered a loud cry and said, "Father, into your hands I commend my spirit."

Luke 23:46

He lost everything that I would hold
And have held dear: his family, his friends,
The approbation of his Church and State,
His last two coins, his clothes—and even and much
Worse—his sense that God was with him, and that
All his anguish mattered. You can suffer
Losing almost anything of value
If at least you know that somehow, somewhere,
Somebody you love has wrung release
From it, has been set free to savor life
Because you gave your own.
But here—no sign,
No moment's ease of darkness or of pain
For seeming nothing offered up. With his
Last breath he will let God create where he
Cannot: "Into your hands I give my life."

I think of this in Holy Week, reflecting
On Jerusalem. His tomb is empty.
You can visit it.

Into your hands, my Rescuer, my Guide, I give my life.

Epilogue

Much to my amazement, I am a pastor again, at another parish. The healing combination of counseling and medication, the support of my family and friends, and the gracious care of God I experienced through prayer convinced me to try again. I know that I will always have to wage this fight against depression, but now I am not disabled by the illness. It has, in fact, made me a wiser human being.

I must depend on God and human love as I never have before, and in some mysterious way it feels wonderful to do just that.

Additional Resources for Spiritual Growth

'Shua
William Burke, with drawings by Mary Southard, C.S.J.
Fr. Burke imagines the story of the life of Jesus told through the eyes of a childhood friend, a friend who—in the end—is not a believer in Jesus as Messiah, but loves him still. (103 page paperback, $8.95; 60-minute video with Discussion Guide, $39.95)

The Evangelists Speak for Themselves
William Burke
Fr. Burke "becomes" each of the four evangelists, who appear before a contemporary audience to explain the background and meaning of each of the gospels. (Mark and Matthew: 75-minute video with Discussion Guide, $49.95; Luke: 45-minute video with Discussion Guide, $39.95; John: 55-minute video with Discussion Guide, $39.95)

From Grief to Grace
Images for Overcoming Sadness and Loss
Helen R. Lambin
A collection of images that assist people in naming, processing and overcoming grief caused by illness, a loved one's death, a job loss or similar difficult situations. (96 page paperback, $8.95)

The Characters Within
Befriending Your Deepest Emotions
Joy Clough, R.S.M.
Explores the deepest human feelings, fears and motivations. Anguish, Blame, Delight, Exhilaration, Humility, Revenge, Vulnerability, Wonder and 50 other emotions come alive through these whimsical, anthropomorphic, evocative reflections. (160 page paperback, $9.95)

Everyday People, Everyday Grace
Daily Meditations for Busy Christians
George R. Szews
Brief stories of ordinary people experiencing God's grace in their everyday lives, coupled with a carefully chosen scripture quotation for each day of the year. (368 page paperback, $9.95)

**Available from booksellers or call
800-397-2282 in the U.S. or Canada.**